YOUR WEBSITE SUCKS

HERE'S HOW TO FIX IT

BRIAN HALL

ECRU PRESS

ISBN: 979-8-9872999-0-6 (Paperback edition)

ISBN: 979-8-9872999-1-3 (Ebook edition)

CONTENTS

INTRODUCTION

Why you should read this book

The chapters that follow will help you diagnose and fix issues with your website. Some of these issues may be obvious to you. Others may be completely off your radar.

By "issues" I mean anything that makes visitors to your site feel confused, frustrated, or simply underwhelmed. With the help of this book, you'll have the knowledge to make low-risk, high-impact improvements that create a seamless user experience.

When you do this, you'll see more visitors convert, whether that means making a purchase, signing up for your software, or filling out a form to talk with your sales team. As you're probably well aware, the more visitors you convert, the more money you make from the same amount of traffic.

So assuming you *have* a website, and it's important to your business (or overall happiness), it's worth checking to see if it violates any of the tried-and-true principles outlined in this book.

Each chapter focuses on a single common problem. If you happen to notice it on your site, I'll tell you how to fix it. (Alternatively, if you find you're in the clear, pat yourself on the back.)

This book won't get into the technical considerations of implementing updates to a website—the ins and outs are far too vast and fast-changing to capture in a single document.

It also won't go into specifics about how to use analytics tools to quantify visitor behavior, though there are a few suggestions on how to get started with them.

It doesn't delve deep into research and theory regarding the behavioral psychology of why people use websites the way they do. Instead, it relies on obvious, uncontroversial observations about basic emotions to make its case.

The focus is on easily identifying issues that are worth your attention and fixing them with as little effort as possible. Simple as that.

Work your way through the whole book and you will be the proud proprietor of the rarely-observed Website That Doesn't Suck.

Why you should listen to me

Since 2016 I've specialized in conversion optimization—the marketing practice of using data, research, psychology, and experimentation to measurably increase revenue generated by websites.

Along the way I've worked with brands like Udemy, L'Oreal, and Ghirardelli, to name a few. Several hundred experiments later (many of them successful and some not), I've gotten a good sense of what stops website visitors from doing what we want them to do.

That said, you don't have to run a lab to build a better website. Controlled experiments frequently lead to surprising insights, but the fact is most website usability issues can be discovered with just a bit of focused attention and empathy with the visitor.

The challenge is in prioritizing potential issues, and knowing how to fix them. I wrote this book to help you do just that.

How to use this book

All chapters follow the same structure. They open with a section describing a common website problem, offer an explanation of why it's a problem, and then give a series of steps you can take to fix it.

Some of these steps will mention research methods you can use to pinpoint issues and highlight potential solutions - techniques like 5 second tests, user testing, polls, and session recording analysis. You can learn more about these topics by visiting the book's website at https://yourwebsitesucks.fyi/book-resources.

There are two parts to the book: User Experience (UX) and Content. The chapters on UX cover issues with visual layout and interactive components (buttons, forms, menus), while the second half of the book focuses on the words, images, and videos that make up your site (aka content).

Within each part, the chapters are ordered from "extremely critical" to "worth your attention, but not critical."

Finally, each chapter is self-contained. So you can read the book front-to-back, compiling a to-do list as you go, or you can jump around and read in whatever order suits you.

Ready to make your website suck less? Read on.

PART I

UX

1

... BECAUSE IT'S BROKEN

In a perfect world, "Make sure your site isn't broken" would be such a laughably obvious piece of advice that no one would bother putting it in a book.

And yet.

As a guy who gets hired to inspect websites and come up with ways to improve them, I find that about 50% of the time my suggestions start with "Fix these broken things."

Maybe one of your images isn't loading:

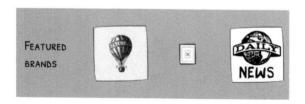

Or your form is missing:

PDF-A-LYZER 5000 TODAY!

Enjoy all of the benefits of PDF-a-lyzer 5000 Pro free for 2 days.

No fine print and no credit card required.

Or a link on your site points to a page that doesn't exist.

Or nothing happens when I click a button.

Or I literally see an error message on the page.

All of these issues are easier to fix, and higher priority, than any other problems you could have. But paying a conversion consultant to find them for you is like hiring an electrician to plug in a toaster. You're better off dealing with them on your own, whether it's through scheduling checks (see below) or asking a friend or colleague to kick the tires on your site.

Here's how to fix it

First, have some sort of early warning system that will alert you if something's keeping visitors from converting. Not all errors will prevent conversion entirely, but when this does happen, you need to know about it and address it as quickly as you can.

The system could be some sort of monitoring function built into your analytics, or it could be as simple as "check leads on a daily basis and make sure they're not at zero."

Visually inspect your highest-traffic pages and any others that are crucial to conversion (e.g., Checkout or Contact Us).

Repeat the process monthly, and whenever you launch a new sitewide change. "Sitewide changes" include:

- A redesign or theme update
- Adding a new tool (like a chat or popup widget)
- Adding a new element to multiple pages (like a banner or sticky footer)

The correct cadence and degree of scrutiny is something you'll dial in over time. Just be sure it's not "never" and "none."

And whatever you do, be sure to spot check your site for "obviously broken stuff" before you pay someone to audit it for you.

2

... BECAUSE IT WON'T CLOSE THE DEAL

I get it: you don't want to be too pushy, too sales-y.

Your website exists to inform, to build awareness and reputation, not just to sell something.

But … you do sell something, right? *Right?*

If so, don't get so caught up in storytelling and education that you neglect to mention the very thing you're storytelling and educating about.

Take the example below. Let's say I've heard good things about a product called Wurkily, so I Google it and land on its homepage. What can I do here?

It's not exactly obvious what they sell—some kind of platform? But if I want to take action, the only option is to Let Them Help.

So I click that button and visit another page. What can I do here?

WE WURK DIFFERENT.

Find out how the Wurkly platform can engage your organization in transformational change.

Not a whole lot. I can read, read some more, or Explore Their Platform.

Fine. I'll go ahead and explore. Here's what I see now:

WHY WORK, WHEN YOU CAN WURK?

Thousands of organizations are using Wurkly to build the future of work.

Automations that Just Wurk.

Explore Automations

"As Chief Work Officer at Flusk, I think about work all day, every day. Wurkly helps."

—Skrob Plemmet, CWO, Flusk

Read More

Transformification

Try Wurkly. Increase your team's output by 1000%.

Find Out How

Here I can ... continue to explore, and continue to read. But if I really want to become a customer, I need to Find Out How.

Except "Find Out How" leads me back to the page I came from. That's frustrating.

So, once again ... what can I do here?

Here's how to fix it

Have a button that represents a single, relevant, clear next step for visitors who want to become customers. Display it throughout your site.

Make it the most prominent button in your header navigation, feature it on your homepage, add it as its own section to other high-traffic pages on your site.

As visitors navigate the site and learn about your product, knowing that this button will take them to the next step will save them time and potential confusion.

For example, if the next step is "Start Free Trial," they will understand they don't have to learn everything about your product before they make a move—just enough to decide if they want to try it.

They're not studying your site for academic purposes— they want to make a decision. A simple, repeated call to action helps them frame the decision and be purposeful in their research.

Give your visitors the gift of this clarity, and they will thank you through conversion.

3

... BECAUSE ITS FORMS ARE TOO LONG

A h, that magical moment.

The moment somebody clicks a button that says Contact Us. (Or Get a Demo, or Start Free Trial, or Subscribe, or Download Report.)

It means they're willing to trade some personal information for what you're offering. It means your website works!

So, don't push your luck.

They *expect* to see a form after that click. And as long as the form is asking for relevant, reasonable info, they'll probably fill it out.

On the other hand, imagine they've searched for "small business lawyer," clicked on a result, and they see this:

COMPLETE THIS FORM AND WE'LL BE IN TOUCH!

First Name

Last Name

Address 1

Address 2

City

State

Zip Code

Email Address

Phone Number

Note

How can we help you?

Submit

The form doesn't even fit on the screen. It asks for an address, phone number, and email—should they expect a call, a message, and a home visit? Do they *want* that?

Imagine they decide to download a white paper and they see this form:

Is it worth sharing your job title and company revenue to read a white paper? Is it even worth the keystrokes it takes to type that information?

If you're like most people, the answer is no.

Here's how to fix it

Consider these two rules of thumb. In general,

- Shorter forms mean more form fills
- You should only ask for information you obviously need

No doubt the sales team wants the name, address, phone number, blood type, and astrological sign of everyone who visits your site. You know, just in case!

But from a visitor's perspective, it should be clear why you're asking for certain information, and what you're going to do with it.

Scheduling a 1-on-1 demo? Company size is probably relevant. Downloading an infographic? Not so much.

Given these rules of thumb, audit every field on every form on your site and ask:

Do we need this? Is it clear to the visitor why we need this?

If not, just remove it.

4

... BECAUSE IT BLOCKS THE USER'S PATH

When you added that chat widget, you placed it unassumingly in the bottom right of the user's screen:

So when you decided to try out that discount-for-an-email-opt-in widget, you put it safely in the bottom left:

There's plenty of space left over for visitors to read your amazing copy, marvel at your striking visuals, click your irresistible buttons.

Except on mobile.

On mobile, your various widgets are scrunched together till they take up 57% of thumb-reachable screen real estate. Which sucks for visitors who don't want to engage with the widgets. Which is most visitors.

This is a good reminder that there's a very fine line between "annoying to the users" and "costly to the business."

And that line gets extra fine where the widgets meet a button or link that's tied to revenue.

Like, say, Add to Bag:

or Schedule a Demo:

Covering up these buttons is like putting yellow police tape around your cash register and asking customers to crawl under it. It's like answering a sales call and saying "Oh hey thanks for reaching out, lemme put you on hold for a minute."

Some people will deal with it. It won't drive your revenue all the way down to zero. But it sucks.

Here's how to fix it

Decide what these widgets are actually worth to your business.

The most rigorous way to find out is an A/B test that removes the widget for 50% of visitors. You can also try turning it off for a month to see if anything drastic happens.

Then, assuming your sales don't go to zero, choose one of the following options. (They're ordered from most to least drastic, so pick the first one you're comfortable with.)

- Remove the widgets from the site entirely
- Remove the widgets, but integrate their functionality into the site navigation
- Remove the widgets on pages where conversions happen
- Remove the widgets on pages where conversions happen, for mobile visitors only
- Minimize the widgets on pages where conversions happen, for mobile visitors only

5

... BECAUSE IT DOESN'T WORK ON MOBILE

No matter what your business is, I assure you that your customers use smartphones.

So if you haven't updated your styling since 1997, it's time to hire a web designer so they can make sure that the mobile version is readable on a small screen, unlike this:

… and make sure that the elements on the page don't overlap each other in weird, illegible ways, like this:

… and that everything fits on the screen:

WE'LL MANAGE YOUR AS:

At Gerbson, Brylocke and Flarkley Associates, asset management is our only priority.

We can guarantee that you'll get careful attention and expert guidance in every aspect of your financial journey.

CONTACT US

... so nobody has to scroll right to read it all:

⌐ MANAGE YOUR ASSETS

ison, Brylocke and Flarkley
tes, asset management is our
ority.

guarantee that you'll get careful
in and expert guidance in every
of your financial journey.

CONTACT US

Other issues you should check for:

- Excessive space between sections
- Links or buttons that are too close together
- Menus that are off-center

Here's how to fix it

The list above is a good starting point for a mobile-friendliness audit. But please, just pay an expert to diagnose and fix your issues. Once that's complete, all you have to do is:

- Add "Review mobile experience" to your checklist for launching site updates
- Check conversion rates by device every few months, and investigate any devices with an abnormally low conversion rate

That's it! You can now rest assured that nobody will angrily throw their phone into a lake after seeing your website.

And as we all know, "not throwing your phone into a lake" is the first step toward conversion.

6

... BECAUSE IT LEAVES VISITORS HANGING

W ith all the effort you spend getting my attention and bringing me to your site, I'd think you would want to guide me in the direction of a purchase, wherever I happen to wander. But no.

You entice me with the promise of stylish yet comfortable pumps, but when I decide to order a pair in size 7, you leave me with nothing to click, nowhere to go.

There's no "Notify me when it's in stock" button or options to "Reserve your pair" or "Try this instead." Just existential despair.

All day comfort!

$189

Please select a size
5 | 6 | 7 | 8 | 9 | 10 | 11 | 12

Add to Bag

You urge me to watch the cinematic masterpiece that is your Product Overview Video ... okay, fine.

PEERLESS PRODUCTIVITY

PLEASE WATCH OUR PRODUCT OVERVIEW VIDEO!!!

But when it ends, I'm alone in a darkened theater, awkwardly holding a bag of stale popcorn. And when I close the window, I'm staring at the same "Watch Our Video!!!" button I just clicked.

PEERLESS PRODUCTIVITY

THANK YOU FOR WATCHING OUR PRODUCT OVERVIEW VIDEO!!

Here's how to fix it

Open your analytics tool and look at a list of all your pages, ranked from most-visited to least-visited.

Set the date range to the last month or two.

Open each of the most-visited pages in your browser and ask yourself, "What do I *want* visitors to do here?" Then confirm that there's a clear and logical way to do just that.

If there is, you should feel relieved—maybe even a little smug. If not, add a button, a form, a new section, etc. Whatever it takes.

Repeat this process, inspecting each page for a clear next step and adding one if necessary. Work down the list until you reach the pages with very few views—at this point you've hit the point of diminishing returns, and can consider the project completed.

When you're done, you'll have a website with no dead ends, much less confusion, and fewer visitors who exit in frustration.

7

... BECAUSE IT GIVES ME TOO MANY OPTIONS

Offer me 10% off and I'm grateful.

Offer me 10% off plus a $30 discount and I appreciate it, but you're making me do math. Do I want the 10% *before* the $30 or after?

Offer me 10% off, plus a $30 discount, plus a $30 rebate, and now I'm just wondering what you're up to.

And yet:

It's true that people love discounts, and that you'll probably see an increase in sales when you offer one.

But it's also true that nobody much cares to do math in their heads in order to choose from competing discount options. Especially before they've even decided whether they want to buy.

This "pile of promos" model is mostly an e-commerce problem, but SaaS sites put their own spin on it.

Here's a collection of buttons from the homepage of a data privacy product:

I appreciate the choose-your-own-adventure spirit of this offering, but how am I to know which path makes the most sense for me?

If I choose a plan, do I still get a free trial? If I start a free trial, I can always Talk to Sales later ... right?

Here's another button collection:

What's the difference between these actions, and how should I choose?

If I get a quote, can I not get a demo as well, and vice versa? And isn't requesting a demo ... a way of contacting you?

This presentation is a problem not just because being unclear or redundant is poor form. The real issue is the very likely chance that I'll simply opt to leave your site rather than expend mental energy deciding which button I should click.

Here's how to fix it

Do the work for your visitors.

Which discount applies to the *majority* of shoppers? Share that one first, and share the others only within a specific context (e.g., only visitors to the Balkan clocks section will be notified that Bulgarian grandfather clocks are 10% off).

Which path should *most* customers follow? Make that the easiest option for them to take. Other options can be secondary—make them smaller, or give them a transparent background so they're less noticeable. Or make them text links, or even push them to the footer.

Just because you make the other buttons smaller, or move them to the footer, doesn't mean nobody will find and use them.

But it does mean that *most* visitors will take the action that's appropriate for ... most visitors. And nobody will give up and leave because you made them think too hard.

8

... BECAUSE IT ASKS FOR TOO MUCH, TOO SOON

S eriously, we just met. I don't know you.

And you're asking me to tell you where I live, enable notifications, and subscribe to your newsletter ... all at once? Before I can even have a look around?

It's not gonna happen.

Imagine you enter a physical store and the owner accosts you at the door. He asks for your name, address, and phone number, then tries to sign you up for his customer loyalty program. Oh, and he wants to send you unsolicited promotions based on your location whenever he feels like it.

You'd probably leave the store at the first opportunity. Politeness might dictate that you promise to "think about it" and maybe pretend to look at a couple items before making your escape.

There's no such opportunity on your website, though. Visitors can (and will) simply close the tab and go elsewhere.

Here's how to fix it

Popups and intrusions take up valuable screen real estate, so make them pay rent.

Don't include them on your site unless you've measured their value and decided that the overall impact on revenue justifies how annoying they are.

As mentioned previously, figuring this out could involve running an experiment where you hide the widget for 50% of visitors. But simply turning it off for a month will give you an idea of whether it's actually crucial to your business.

Of course, it's possible that you're not even measuring or monitoring the impact of the widget to begin with. If that's the case, your approach to displaying it should default to the setting of Not Annoying.

That might mean asking visitors to enable notifications only after they have engaged with your site.

It might mean triggering your newsletter popup *only* after a visitor has spent 30 seconds on the page.

It might mean not asking visitors to enable location services at all, or at least not until it's clear why you're asking.

In the absence of evidence to the contrary, I am hereby giving you permission to assume that "Don't harass visitors" is the optimal strategy.

9

... BECAUSE ITS FORM FIELDS ARE A LABYRINTHINE NIGHTMARE

Your site doesn't make money unless visitors fill out forms.

They come to learn, to compare, to consider, maybe even to admire your content. But sooner or later they have to fill out a form, whether they want to check out, contact you, or sign up for something.

You know this, so you've already ensured that your forms aren't too long. (Good job!) But even with a short form, where all the info you're requesting is perfectly reasonable, it's possible to confuse and alienate your visitors.

Let's talk about labels and placeholder text.

Placeholder text is whatever a visitor sees inside an input field before they start typing. "Email address" and "Password" are placeholder text in this form:

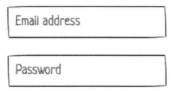

In the above form, the placeholder text also functions as a label, i.e., they indicate what the user is supposed to type into the input field.

You can also use placeholder text to provide suggestions (note that the labels sit above the input fields):

You shouldn't do either.

Using placeholder text introduces all sorts of usability challenges.

Here's the biggest one. Once a user starts filling out the form, there's a very good chance they will completely forget what information is supposed to go in what field. If they make a mistake, they can't easily go back and correct it.

What's wrong with this form submission?

Brian		Hail
		This field is required.

The answer is, "The second form field is supposed to contain an email address," but an equally fair response would be, "No clue, how am I supposed to know?"

Even when you do have labels, as in the second example, you're better off leaving out the placeholder text. For one, it adds visual clutter. It's also hard for low-sight visitors to read.

On top of that, our eyes are drawn to empty fields, especially when our immediate-term goal is to fill them out. It's not clear to all users that the placeholder text must be replaced. Visitors may skip filled-out-looking fields entirely—until your angry red validation message corrects them.

Here's how to fix it

Put labels above form fields. Be sure they're closer to the field
they correspond to than to other fields in the form. Leave out
placeholder text. Do this:

Name

Email address

Password

It might not be as cute or stylish, but it will help visitors fill out
the form more accurately and easily. Which is what we all want.

10

... BECAUSE ITS NAVIGATION IS OVERWHELMING

W e get it. You have a huge website with lots of pages.

But here's a little known internet fact: there's no law saying your top navigation menu has to contain a link to every single page on your site.

If anything, there's a general principle that says it *shouldn't*.

I seek out your navigation because I want to get a sense of what's available on your site, or because I already know what I'm looking for and I want to access it.

In either case, the ideal experience is being presented with a handful of options, one of which seems to be what I'm looking for.

If it requires more than one click to reach my destination, that's not a problem—as long as *figuring out what to click* is easy every step of the way.

A giant list of options, on the other hand, does not inspire confidence. Instead, it elicits confusion and overwhelm. It asks me to *work*.

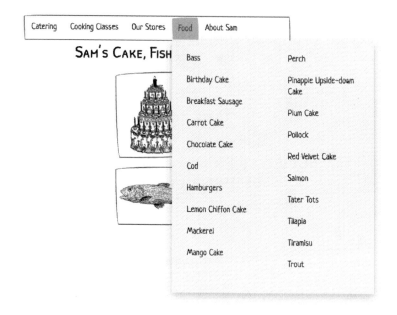

I can scan for the exact word I'm looking for, but there's no guarantee that a word on the screen will match the word in my head.

So I might have to scan several times, then start over at the top,
reading each option, one by one, to decide if it's relevant to my
intention. (This is assuming I even remember what I was looking
for after 20 seconds of staring at a screen full of text.)

On a good day, I might have the patience for this task. Or I might
opt out of using the navigation bar, but continue to look for what
I want using search or on-page links.

But most likely I'll stare for a few seconds, shake my head, and
close the tab. Off to pursue less painful endeavors.

Here's how to fix it

The guiding principle here is "make the next click easy."

If your top-level navigation has 8+ items, eliminate as many as possible. This will make it a lot easier for visitors to figure out which one to click.

If that means using dropdown navigation, that's fine!

But if one of your dropdowns has 8+ items, again: eliminate as many as possible, so it's easier for visitors to figure out which one to click.

If that means linking to category pages, that's fine! Category pages are a great way to organize content-heavy websites. And if you sell a dozen different cakes, ten kinds of fish, and an assortment of other edible items, there's no need to jumble them all together in a dropdown. Just provide links to browse cakes, fish, or other foods.

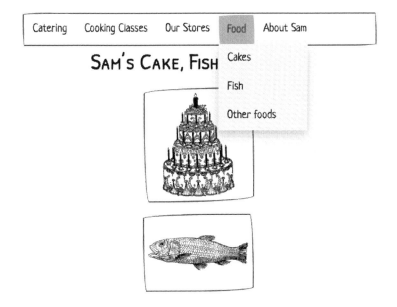

It might take a few clicks to find the exact page they're looking for, and that's not a problem. Nobody minds a few clicks as long as they feel confident they're headed in the right direction.

11

... BECAUSE IT ONLY WORKS FOR SOME PEOPLE

Your site is gorgeous. Looks amazing—to me, anyway.

But how does it look to the visually impaired? Can they even read your headings?

How does it *sound* to the millions of internet users—visually impaired, learning disabled, or non-native English speakers—who use a screen reader program to speak the contents of the site out loud?

The answer is probably, "Like a hot mess." The good news is that a few straightforward fixes can greatly improve your site's accessibility, and *they're good for conversion too*.

Here's how to fix it

Use alt text

Alt text is a short snippet of text that describes an image. It's invisible to visitors browsing your site visually, but it's available to those who can't see images.

Make alt text concise and descriptive, and make sure anybody with the ability to upload images to your site understands the importance of adding it.

Simplify your primary navigation

"If you link to it, they will come" … said no one, ever.

You already know that cramming too many options into your top navigation does sighted visitors no favors—it offers an over-whelming number of options.

But it's even worse for people using screen readers (an assistive technology that speaks the contents of the screen to visitors). They will hear *the entire navigation* read out loud before getting to the page contents.

So just put your most relevant, most-visited options in the navigation. Kick the rest to the footer.

Label your form fields

You already know that using placeholder text to label form fields makes it confusing for sighted visitors. What's worse is that it leaves screen reader users without any context at all.

Just add labels. Put them right above the input field they're describing.

Make your copy clear and concise

If a page is full of convoluted, abstruse language, sighted visitors will mostly just ignore the copy altogether. (Not good.)

But visitors using screen readers will have to *listen to it all.* (Even worse.)

They don't get to enjoy the benefit of your fancy animations and visual effects. Just that overlong, mediocre copy.

Load up your homepage or top landing page. Try reading it out loud. Or take 15 minutes to install and try out a screen reader.

The parts where you cringe, or start getting bored—those are where you need to make edits.

12

… BECAUSE IT LOOKS JUST LIKE EVERYONE ELSE'S

I can't predict what trend will be omnipresent across business websites as you read this, but I guarantee there will be one. There always is.

In the early days of the internet, clip art and animated GIFs were everywhere. Then at one point, everyone's site had a series of stock photos—actors dressed like businesspeople, smiling and shaking hands. Just like real businesspeople do.

The e-commerce world went through a "short, looping, silent video on autoplay" phase at one point. And in the late 2010s, every SaaS website inexplicably had the same flat, generic vector art people on their homepage.

SaaSlifi.er

Redefining SaaS for SaaS

Learn More

Whatever trend you're seeing on everyone else's website this quarter, you may be inclined to assume that they're doing it because it works, and that you should do the same.

The fact is, following trends like this doesn't help me understand your product or how it can solve my problems. It doesn't instill trust, or paint a picture of a desirable outcome. And it certainly doesn't set you apart from the competition.

Here's how to fix it

Remind yourself that unless you have good evidence, you don't know if your competitors' website strategy is working. It's quite possible *they* don't even know if it's working.

So if you have a stylistic element or feature on your website that's just there because it's common in your industry, consider removing it.

It may be possible to measure visitor engagement in order to inform this decision, but it's okay to trust yourself too. Just ask: does this help visitors understand the product? Does it help set us apart?

Clearly the answer is "no" for generic stock photos and uninspired illustrations.

Get rid of them.

Instead, focus on visuals that help visitors make a decision. Show the product in use, add diagrams to help explain important concepts, and paint a picture of the outcome successful users can expect to achieve.

You'll need to update this content from time to time, as your product (or customer) changes. But you *won't* have to update it every time a new design trend comes along.

13

... BECAUSE IT WON'T SIT STILL

L et's talk about carousels, those dynamic elements that rotate between multiple images, and sometimes multiple headlines and buttons.

To you, they might seem fun and engaging. The truth is, they're distracting, they look like ads, they're hard to click on, and they're problematic for people using screen readers.

For all these reasons, they're bad for conversion and user experience. This is a well-worn topic among UX and conversion professionals.

But you still have one, don't you? You might even be putting two on the same page.

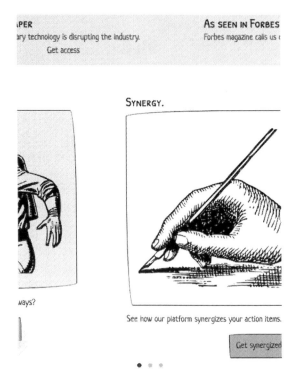

SYNERGY.

See how our platform synergizes your action items.

Get synergized

For the sake of conversions, and your visitors' eyeballs, please stop.

Here's how to fix it

Replace your carousel with a single, static element.

Use the combination of message, call to action, and (optional) image that is most relevant to most of your customers.

Put everything else below it. You're done.

Maybe that's not an option because you don't know which message is most relevant. Or your team can't agree which message is most relevant.

In this case, test it.

One idea is to hire an online service to run a "preference test." This is a market research survey that asks a qualified panel of participants to evaluate multiple options and choose the most compelling.

If your team can't agree on the single most important message your visitors need to hear ... and isn't willing to let your audience decide for them ... well, we tried, didn't we?

Sucks for you. And your visitors.

14

... BECAUSE IT'S ILLEGIBLE

All the snappy website copy in the world won't persuade me to buy … if I can't read it.

Imagine the sense of anticipation I feel as I click a link to visit your site, and how it gives way to consternation when I encounter white text over a light background image.

Consider the pain you put me through when I visit on mobile, only to encounter text so small I have to pinch and zoom to read it.

There's plenty of ambiguity in the world, but I'm pretty confident that your website makes more money when people can read it.

Here's how to fix it

Don't have text with a font size smaller than 16 pixels anywhere on your site. If you find yourself needing to use a smaller font to fit everything in, say less.

And whenever you put text over images, have a designer add a transparent overlay so the copy stands out:

Or give the text box a high-contrast background color:

These minor design tweaks ensure that the copy and images you've worked so hard to create don't negate each other, confusing visitors in the process.

And a less confused visitor is more likely to buy.

15

... BECAUSE IT DOESN'T WORK WITH ADBLOCK

I t's not your fault.

You didn't turn the internet into a cesspool of scammy clickbait promotions.

You haven't glutted your website with so many trackers, banners, and ads that people have to join the hundreds of millions of users who employ ad blocking technology.

Someone else did that.

But it's done, and those adblock users come to your site, and it looks broken to them.

DOWNLOAD A FREE TRIAL OF
PDF-A-LYZER 5000 TODAY!

Enjoy all of the benefits of PDF-a-lyzer 5000 Pro free for 2 days.

No fine print and no credit card required.

There *is* a form on this page, but it's being generated by a highly popular marketing automation tool ... which just so happens to be on the default block list of a highly popular privacy plugin.

Current estimates indicate that about 40% of internet users are browsing with an ad blocker. Are you okay with 40% of visitors being unable to fill out your form?

Here's how to fix it

Install an ad blocker or two and visit your site.

Does everything work? Great, crisis averted, see you next chapter.

If anything is missing or broken, though, you've got work to do.

At a minimum, provide a fallback experience that visitors see when a privacy tool blocks part of your site. A message like this:

We use Formy McFormerson™, a trusted third-party tool, to manage form submissions.

It looks like AdBlock or another privacy extension is keeping it from working—please disable any privacy tools and reload the page.

If you read that and think, "Ugh, I don't want to put that on my website" … well, I'm with you. Much better to have a site that works for 100% of visitors, on the first try.

This may lead you to reevaluate your tools and plugins, and to open up a few tickets with your dev team. It will cost time and money.

But hiding your forms and other key content from 40% of visitors also costs money.

You know what you have to do.

16

... BECAUSE IT'S SLOW

Nobody likes to wait.

Specifically, nobody likes to wait when they're not expecting it.

If you're at the grocery store, you expect to have a couple people in line in front of you. Not a big deal. But if there are eight people ahead of you, that sucks.

It's much the same with websites. When you visit one, you expect to see some text, and maybe an image, within a few seconds. You expect to be able to interact with it after a couple more seconds. If you can't, that sucks.

So if your website locks up for 20 seconds or more before it becomes usable, I guarantee people are hitting the back button and moving on to their next distraction.

And the ones who stick around have internalized the notion that your site—and possibly the product behind it —is slow and unreliable.

Here's how to fix it

First of all, hold yourself to reasonable standards.

You may have read headlines making bold claims like "Just a 100-millisecond delay in load time hurt conversion rates by up to 7%."

That's a great headline, probably got lots of clicks. It doesn't apply to you.

Set a goal for your page load time based on what your visitors expect, and what your technical capabilities will allow.

How fast do your competitors' sites load? If you're in the same ballpark, it's probably fine.

If the page where most visitors enter the site takes more than 15 seconds to become usable, or if it's noticeably slower than your competitors, spend a couple days' worth of developer time to try and speed it up.

For most marketing sites, this boils down to "Install a speed optimization plugin, compress images, and be done with it."

Let someone else dump tons of money into trying to be the fastest site in the world. As long as you're not losing visitors in droves, you should settle for "not terrible" and move on.

17

... BECAUSE IT ASKS UNNECESSARY QUESTIONS

I magine you meet someone new and ask where they're from.

"Paris," they reply.

"Oh, cool," you say. "And what country are you from?"

The conversation isn't likely to go much further. They'll think you're either dumb or trolling.

But you'd never ask that followup question, because there's obviously no reason to. You know better.

Your website, on the other hand ...

Take a look at this checkout screen:

PAYMENT METHOD

Credit / Debit Card

Credit Card Number

Credit Card Type

- ✓ Please Select Credit Card Type
- **Visa**
- **Mastercard**
- **American Express**

January | 2023

Security Code

Fun fact, the first digit of a credit card number tells you what type of card it is: 3 for American Express, 4 for Visa, 5 for MasterCard, 6 for Discover.

So there's no need to ask.

This unnecessary question is annoying to me, and it's off-putting even to people who *don't* spend their free time researching the arcana behind credit card numbers. Because they shop online all the time, and almost no other site asks for this info.

You might introduce similar friction if you have an address auto-complete function. (The one that asks visitors to start typing their address, then select the correct one from a dynamically populated dropdown box.)

Once I select that address, you've got my city, state, and zip code. Please don't ask me to type them in manually.

When I start filling out your form, it's because I'm excited to do business with you! But when you make that process slower and more frustrating than it needs to be, my excitement starts to wane, and doubt creeps in. I start to wonder if every interaction with you will be this annoying. Push it too far, and I'll just close the tab.

Here's how to fix it

You've already made sure that your forms aren't too long.

Take another look at every input you require visitors to complete and ask, is there any way to get this information other than making them type it?

If you don't have to ask, don't ask. If you do have to ask, but *not yet*, ask later.

And if you can derive the answer from something they've already told you, just do that.

18

... BECAUSE IT'S TRYING TO IMPRESS ME

J ust because you can, doesn't mean you should.

You *can* use fancy styling to cause every element of your page to slide in, slide up, slide down, or spiral onto the screen as you scroll.

I'll be honest: back in 2009, when I first saw this kind of animation, my response was, "Ooh."

So I understand if you had the same reaction when your website design came in for review and you saw all those moving pieces.

Since 2009, though, I've seen something else. I've seen lots of humans using websites, and when humans use websites they like to scroll and scan.

And all those impressive animation effects mean you can scroll, but you can't scan.

WHY WO

Thousands of organiza

As Chief Work Officer at
al day, every da

—Sarah Pieron

Read

These effects are all over the internet because they look impressive to the people who pay website designers.

Not because they have any effect on website visitors, at least beyond slowing them down, frustrating them, or possibly creating the impression that the site is broken.

Here's how to fix it

Give your homepage one last, lingering, slow scroll. Let out a wistful "ooh." Then kill the animations.

What you'll get is a page that feels fast, and facilitates the finding of information. Which is what people came to your website for!

19

... BECAUSE IT'S TOO CONSISTENT

I t's so nice to bring order to chaos.

Accordingly, each element of your website is drawn from a comprehensive design system, ensuring no erratic, out-of-place details to distract from the flawless unity of your masterful vision.

Some websites have a slapped-together, design-by-committee look and feel that distracts, confuses, and undermines trust. Not yours!

Bad news, though: it's possible to take this too far.

For example: in the quest to provide a consistent experience across all popups on your site, you might find yourself creating something like this:

"Click 'Cancel' to cancel cancelling." At least that's how I read this instruction—what about you?

"Confirm/Cancel" as default popup options make sense for *most* actions. Send email? Confirm. Update profile photo? Eh, cancel.

It's just this one action where things break down.

But if every other popup on the site has the same two buttons, what are you supposed to do—change this one? Break the consistency of the entire site?

Yes.

Here's how to fix it

Have a design system and be consistent with it. Just be willing to make exceptions.

You don't have to throw out the harmonious patterns you've created. 99% of the time they will be the right answer.

And a regular practice of user testing, session recording analysis, and auditing chat logs for user frustration will point you to the 1% of cases where you need to break with convention.

So: be consistent.

But also: listen to your users. And be willing to break the rules in order to address their confusion.

PART II

CONTENT

20

... BECAUSE IT'S UNCLEAR WHAT YOU'RE EVEN SELLING

E very single visitor to your site is a victory, and an opportunity.

Out of all the queries I might have typed into the search engine, I chose one that points to one of your pages. Out of all the search results, I clicked on yours.

Amazing.

Maybe I even arrived with a measure of trust in and familiarity with you or your site. Maybe I Googled you because a friend mentioned your product favorably. Even more amazing!

Unless what I see upon landing is completely inscrutable.

Unless, after developing an interest in self-hosted alternatives to Google Drive / Dropbox, and talking to a trusted friend who is an expert in the field, and finding out that he uses a thing called Flurb for file storage, and excitedly typing "flurb" into the search engine and clicking the top result ... unless after all that, I see this:

Flurb

GOLGI 2.7 IS HERE!

Why upgrade to Golgi 2.7? We've implemented a proprietary data architecture format that makes compliance monitoring and reporting easier.

Learn More

What is Golgi? Why should I care about a new data architecture format? "Makes compliance monitoring and reporting easier"— easier than what? What am I looking at?

The fact that there's no visual representation of the product is a problem we'll address in a future chapter. Our concern here is more fundamental: there's no indication on the page of what the product even *is*.

Here's how to fix it

Make sure the top section of your homepage clearly communicates what your product is, and what problem it solves.

(For bonus points, you should also convey who it's for and what makes it different from alternatives.)

Test and improve on this language until it's as elegant as possible.

If you have an exciting announcement to make, use a narrow banner at the top of the page, or a section further down the page, or maybe an annoying popup. Or even all three.

But remember that (a) nobody is as excited about this announcement as you, and (b) new visitors have to understand what you do before they can celebrate amazing news.

21

... BECAUSE IT DOESN'T TELL ME WHAT I'M GETTING

Once upon a time there was a viral video of a teenager trying to trade a "mystery box" for a $6.50 video game at a pawn shop. The shop owner says no— "Can't run a business on a gamble."

Spoiler alert, there's $500 in the box.

But the shop owner's right. It doesn't make sense to accept an unspecified offer from someone you don't know.

So as much as I might want to sign up for this champagne delivery box:

THE PARTY BOX!

Time to party! This box includes two sparkling wines to liven up your next gathering.

You'll receive:

- Complimentary sipping glass
- Your choice of two wines
- Pairing guide

Order now

… I'm not going to click Order Now without knowing the details. "Two wines"—are those cans, boxes, or bottles? Splits or demis? The page doesn't say.

I might be persuaded to sign up for this playbooks-as-a-service platform:

… but when I click "Try Free" here's what I see:

This product has different plans and pricing tiers. Which one am I getting for the 7-day trial? What happens after the trial ends? What's in the mystery box?

Here's how to fix it

If you have an e-commerce website, make sure you include thorough product details for everything in your store. Dimensions, volume, weight, quantity, color, materials.

If you have a SaaS product and offer a free trial, make sure you tell visitors what plan they're trialing and what happens after the trial is over.

Either way, consider adding a small, unobtrusive popup to key internal pages on your site. Just ask one question: "What's missing from this page?"

After a few weeks, if you've left out any essential information, some kind-hearted soul will take the time to type it into the popup.

There are so many reasons for losing conversions on your website, and lots of them are out of your control. Don't let "I dunno what yer selling" be one of them.

22

... BECAUSE IT WON'T SHOW ME THE GOODS

Y ou and I know that you actually have a product. (Or a service. Or both.)

It exists, it solves problems, it's wonderful. People love it.

But we also know that there are unscrupulous types out there who advertise (and even sell) products that *don't* exist, or that fail to live up to expectations.

And the poor souls visiting your website, they don't know you like I know you. They don't know how truly scrupulous you are. They're on constant alert for scams.

The easiest way to show them that you have a real product is to ... show them the product. So why don't you?

It's embarrassingly common to land on the homepage of a SaaS product and find plenty of weird illustrated people, or stock photos, but no images of the product itself. This despite the fact that people come to these pages for the *sole purpose* of learning about the product.

This issue is less common in e-commerce, where you're generally obligated to show at least a single picture of what you're selling. But from a visitor's perspective, one grainy photo might as well be nothing.

When you're secretive about what your product actually looks like, you force visitors to take a leap of faith. Before they engage further with your site, they have to decide, "Well, okay, this is *probably* real …"

But for every visitor who decides to trust you, how many are just closing the tab and moving on with their lives?

Here's how to fix it

Prominently display images of your product on your website. Show people *what they'll see after becoming customers.*

For SaaS products, this typically looks like screenshots. If you're selling a payment platform, show images of earnings reports and checkout screens.

This imagery will communicate the following: "If you become a customer, you'll be looking at earnings reports and checkout screens." But beyond that, it unambiguously says, "We have an actual product that works."

For e-commerce, show products from multiple angles, in context, with good lighting, and on a human model where appropriate. Use high resolution, zoomable images.

If what you sell doesn't have much to show for itself visually—like services, or an API—this gets trickier. It's not impossible, though.

Ask yourself, "What will this website visitor be looking at *after* they become a customer?"

Is it your smiling face on a Zoom call? A monthly report? Server logs that tell them their request latency has gone down? Slap a photo of *that* on your website.

23

... BECAUSE IT WON'T STOP BRAGGING

Y ou know and I know that your product is amazing.

Everyone who tries it loves it. Very intelligent people are talking about it.

It makes sense that you want to communicate this to your website visitors. But is it possible you're being ... a little heavy handed about it?

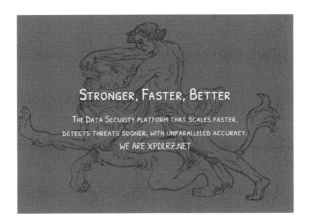

Here's the thing: Most people coming to your website don't know you. And they don't necessarily trust you yet.

So when you tell them how strong and fast you are, all they really learn is that you're self-centered.

It's great that you've developed a broad suite of solutions, won some big-name customers, and made the news recently. But the time to bring this up is probably after explaining what you can do for your website visitors:

THE DIGITAL EXCELLENCE PLATFORM

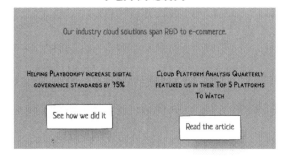

It's cool you've gotten some press, but is sharing that really more important than ... offering your actual product to the people who came to your website to learn about it?

Noodles By Mail

The *premier* mail order noodles service.

Trying to increase your access to noodles without leaving the house? Try Noodles By Mail and get your first 0.3kg of noodles at a 17% discount!

Here's how to fix it

Think fast: What problem causes people to seek you out in the first place? How does it *feel* to have that problem? What is their life like after you solve it for them?

Talk about this on your homepage.

One of the best headlines I've ever seen was from a fitness course and community focused on increasing mobility in middle aged men.

They have over a hundred hours of courses from instructors with years of experience, but they don't mention this immediately on their homepage. Instead, they lead with this:

Don't die without exploring what your body is truly capable of.

On a slightly less dramatic note, here's a headline from a real-life online marketing platform:

Build your brand, sell online - all in one place.

Notice how both examples use words like "you" and "your"? If your website copy uses these words, you're on the right track.

There's no shortcut to convincing people to love your product. You have to get them to try it first.

And the way to get them to try it is to demonstrate that you understand their problems.

24

... BECAUSE IT'S A BAMBOOZLE

Not *literally*—I don't mean you're selling my info without my consent (though some people are) or advertising a product that you'll never deliver (though that happens too).

I'm talking about the way that you promise me something to get me to your site, then fail to keep that promise.

Say I'm searching for an industry veteran to help me steer my startup. I search for "hire startup advisor" and see this result:

hire startup advisor

Ad https://hiringly.com/ ⋮

Hire Freelance Consultants

Hire Vetted and Handpicked Startup
Consultants. Focus On Growing Your
Business, Not Hiring.

That seems like just what I need: a vetted consultant who can help me with strategy. Someone who specializes in startups.

Here's the page I land on:

HIRE A 10X FREELANCE PROJECT MANAGER!

Hiringly.com is the leading platform for hiring talented project managers. Top companies hire Freelance Project Managers from Hiringly.com.

> Hire now!

Sorry, what?

Don't get me wrong; project managers are *so* important. But that's not what I searched for or clicked on.

It's like I sat down to eat at a restaurant and the server is trying to sell me a boat. I don't want a boat.

Here's how to fix it

Make the landing page match the link your visitors clicked.

That's it.

If you're doing SEO, make sure your content actually answers people's questions (don't just write it to please Google).

If you're running ads, make sure you don't buy keywords without having a relevant page to send people to.

If you're running *a lot* of ads, too many to track, and you're really not sure who's landing where or what they're doing when they get there, consider that you may be wasting a lot of money.

And complicating your operations unnecessarily.

And bamboozling tons of unwitting visitors.

25

... BECAUSE IT'S COLD AND UNFEELING

P eople visit your website to find information. To solve a problem.

If they can't confirm that you've got:

- the product they need,
- with the features they need,
- at a price they can afford

... you'll never sell a thing.

But there's more to a purchase decision than verifying facts.

Your visitors have to stick around long enough to learn all that info, for one thing. And if your site isn't engaging, if it doesn't spark curiosity, they won't.

They have to remember you, too, since they're almost certainly checking out your competition as well.

Not only that, they have to overcome their resistance to (a) spending money and (b) the friction of filling out yet another form.

Curiosity, interest, and motivation don't come from bullet points of product features. These are *feelings,* and your site needs to create them out of the hesitation and doubts your visitors arrive with.

This is hard! Especially if you avoid emotion-stoking language altogether. Take this page:

COLLABORATE EFFECTIVELY

Our platform offers the best way to

- Chat
- Share files
- Conduct meetings
- Track tasks

Use our website, or mobile app. Receive notifications via email or SMS. Integrate with 73 other apps.

Do you have the warm fuzzies? I doubt it. I know I don't.

Here's how to fix it

Name the feelings that bring visitors to your website, and the feelings they're seeking as they start clicking around.

You can incorporate this explicitly—for example, a home security system website with a heading that says, "Peace of mind for your home."

The motivating feelings are worry and insecurity, and the desired feeling is peace of mind.

Or you can incorporate these feelings indirectly—for example, an analytics tool that promises "No more writing awkward SQL queries or waiting for someone to do it for you."

The motivating feeling is frustration, and the desired feeling is autonomy or confidence.

It feels really nice to have your emotional state acknowledged and validated. People pay therapists hundreds of dollars an hour for this experience. Imagine the results if you provide it for free!

If you don't know how your visitors feel

Remember two things:

1. It's okay :)
2. Finding out should be your top priority

The best way to figure this out is to talk to happy customers. Here are two questions you can ask:

- *If our product went away tomorrow, how would you feel?*
- *Take me back to when you first realized you needed a solution for _____. Where were you? What were you feeling?*

This feelings stuff is messy. You won't get a clear, unambiguous answer. You'll need to take some chances and make some educated guesses.

You might feel nervous about adding emotional language to your website. That's perfectly normal because, again, *this stuff is hard.*

… See what I did there?

I did my very best to acknowledge the way you might feel upon reading this chapter. Maybe I got it right, maybe not. But hopefully you appreciate the sincere effort.

Try your best, and your visitors will appreciate your effort too.

26

... BECAUSE IT'S FOR EVERYBODY

Imagine you've successfully bid your way to the first page of results for this very expensive query:

asbestos laywer california

Y ou're paying somewhere between $60 and $450 *per click* on this ad.

Now imagine this is where you take me when I click your ad:

ATTORNEYS HELPING
PEOPLE

Flurxton and Jimbley Associates are the premier law firm for assisting people with legal matters.

Call us today.

Attorneys helping … *people*?

So you've successfully distinguished yourself from lawyers representing insects and robots. But that's it.

Despite the very specific information that I communicated by clicking a very targeted, *very expensive* ad, you're giving no reassurance that you specialize in—or even particularly care about—my unique situation.

Everybody picks on lawyers, though. How about SaaS companies?

Here's a list of homepage headings from several real-life marketing automation (aka "bulk-email sending") platforms:

- Empower your Marketing team and engage your audience with automation
- Big, small, in-house or agency, we've got your business covered
- Marketing Automation for the Modern Marketer
- From Collecting Data to Connecting, Let the Platform Do The Work - Focus on what matters most to you as a marketer

Assuming you're still awake, let's talk about this copy.

We've got a strangely capitalized reference to "your Marketing team" and a mention of "the Modern Marketer," whatever that means.

There's an allusion to "what matters most to you as a marketer" without any detail as to what that might be. And there's the "big, small, in-house or agency" catchall language—a misguided attempt to capture every type of marketer on the planet.

Here's how to fix it

Dare to be just *slightly* different. Seriously, I dare you.

Talk to your happiest customers, find out what they love about your product, and what it is about them that makes you such a great fit.

Then, pluck up your courage and mention this, explicitly, on your website.

Maybe you don't sell to large enterprises. If not, you have my permission to talk about small businesses and highlight why *they* think you're great.

Enterprise visitors to your site will probably leave, as they should.

But small business visitors will feel seen, instead of feeling generic. Intrigued, instead of bored. Reassured, instead of suspicious.

Who knows? They might even feel like buying from you.

27

... BECAUSE IT'S WRITTEN FOR A ROBOT

The most compelling website copy in the world won't help you if nobody reads it. So you need a strategy for bringing people to your site.

Optimizing your content for search engine discovery is one such strategy, which plenty of businesses employ to great success.

And yet.

The highest search ranking in the world won't help you if your copy reads like a pile of machine-generated gibberish.

Like when you use the phrase "foreclosed home" 36 times in a single blog post:

How to buy a Foreclosed Home

Are you looking to buy a foreclosed home? There are pros and cons to each foreclosed home purchase, so before you purchase a foreclosed home be sure to read our definitive guide to buying a foreclosed home!

A foreclosed home is one that is typically owned by a mortgage lender or bank due to

... or when you use the name of a single product seven times in a single paragraph:

Goliath C-100 Truck Parts

Introduced way back in 1994, the Goliath C-100 has become the all-powerful emperor of trucks. And, with our amazing selection of custom-fit Goliath C-100 seat covers, protective Goliath C-100 floor mats, multiple fashionanble (and functional) Goliath C-100 bed covers, durable Goliath C-100 fender flares, and much more, Autostravaganza.net has become the all-powerful emperor of Goliath C-100 truck accessories.

Here's how to fix it

First, consider whether keyword-optimized SEO content is even a valuable strategy for your site.

There are other ways for people to find your website. Maybe they come via social media, or ads, or searching for it by name. If that's how visitors find your site, you have my permission to write content for a human audience.

If you do decide to go for an SEO-optimized content strategy, keep in mind that not all SEO practitioners are created equally.

Shop around, and for each expert you talk to, check out the content they've created for other clients. Does it make your eyeballs bleed?

There's a huge difference in quality between what you get from someone who simply ingests keywords and spits out blog posts vs. someone who's thoughtful about solving your visitors' problems.

With a bit of diligence, you can end up with content that satisfies robots and humans alike.

28

... BECAUSE IT'S INORDINATELY CIRCUMLOCUTORY

In other words, it's wordy.

I know your website visitors are smart. Possibly the smartest people in the world. After all, they've decided to learn more about *your* amazing product.

But they're also humans. They're distracted, hung over, and half-paying-attention to their fifth meeting of the day.

They have ten other tabs open on desktop, and on mobile they're forever feeling the pull of their favorite social media dopamine fix.

They're not about to read pages that look like this:

Aʟʟ THE VESSELS YOU NEED

In the course of a typical day, you will find yourself in need of any number of vessels. Vessels to hold liquids, solid, or even gaseous elements. It's obviously important to have the right vessel for whatever it is you need to store – or pour – but it's also crucial that you have the right size. Luckily, we stock vessels in a wide variety of shapes and sizes, perfectly suited to whatever purpose you might have.

So, how to choose a vessel? There are several factors to consider. First, what is your budget? Once you know how much you're willing to spend on a vessel, you can explore various vessel options and styles. Next up, what type of vessel speaks to you? We firmly believe that there's a vessel for everyone, and if you haven't found yours yet,

They may scan and skim for a minute or so. But not even the most literary minded of your visitors will stick around on a website that reads like a novel.

Here's how to fix it

Zoom out and visually scan your main web pages for the proverbial Wall of Text.

Where you see one, break it up with images, headings, and bullet points.

Next, shorten it. Turn paragraphs into sentences, then turn the sentences into phrases.

You're done when a five-second glance at any section of any page on your site is enough to understand what the content is about.

29

... BECAUSE IT'S LYING TO ME

O ne way to get more people to make a purchase is to provide social proof: evidence that other humans, ideally similar to them, have already made a purchase.

Another tactic is to create a sense of urgency: implying that visitors need to act quickly or they'll miss out on an opportunity.

Deploying these tactics is often as simple as adding some copy or installing a free widget on your site.

For example, if you've built an e-commerce site on any of the popular platforms, you'll have several options for creating "social proof sales popups." They look like this:

And a few lines of custom code will get you "shopping cart urgency messaging":

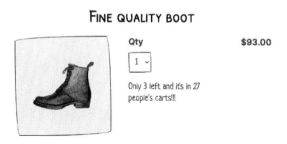

FINE QUALITY BOOT

Qty   **$93.00**

[1 ⌄]

Only 3 left and it's in 27
people's carts!!!

Crucially, you can trigger the sales pop ups even if you're not getting sales. And you can fire up the shopping cart message whether the item is actually scarce or not.

Given that these notifications are based on solid psychological principles of persuasion, and since it's pretty simple to add them to your site, doesn't it make sense to try them out and see if they help?

No. Because they're cheap, dishonest hacks that real humans will see through.

Here's how to fix it

Do not lie to your customers. Even if it increases sales in the short term, do not lie to your customers.

Do not use these tactics if the information they present is not absolutely true.

Even if it *is* true, you should probably avoid them anyway. Plenty of other websites use them dishonestly, and your customers won't necessarily know that you're one of the good guys.

Here are a couple of ethical—and more persuasive— ways to provide social proof:

- Display customer reviews, ideally including a picture of the reviewer
- Use video:
- For e-commerce, add unboxing videos from real customers
- For SaaS products or lead generation, create video case studies and testimonials

As for urgency, it's fine to let visitors know if supplies are limited or an offer will soon expire.

And it's fine to experiment with where and how you present this information.

It's fine to try all sorts of tactics. Just keep in mind that so-called Best Practices, or growth hacks, or plugins and add-ons will not provide you with a moral compass.

It's up to you to decide where to draw the line, and so I beg you: do not lie to your customers.

30

... BECAUSE IT WANTS TO BE A MOVIE

V*ideo is king, right?*

A 2017 study indicated that people in the US watch nearly 6 hours of video per day.

With all those hungry eyeballs, it seems obvious that you should produce a slick, stylish video explaining why your product and company are so amazing. Give it some jaunty background music, a cameo from a retired sports celebrity, and plop it up there at the top of your homepage. Right?

Not so fast.

It pains me to deliver this news, but people do not visit your website with the same goals and mindset they bring to watching reality TV or sports. They're looking for information, not entertainment.

And even the greatest product explainer video of all time, even if it's directed by a five-time Oscar winner, will be ignored by the vast majority of visitors.

A video is not searchable the way plain text is. It's not copy-pasteable. It's not skimmable. It requires turning the volume up.

And most importantly … nobody particularly cares about your cool video except you and your leadership team. Possibly your mom or dad.

Here's how to fix it

If you absolutely must make a video, go ahead. If you've already made one, don't worry—you're certainly not alone.

Just don't stick it at the very top of your homepage.

Instead of relying on a video, focus on crafting a heading, subheading, and (optional) visual that convey what problem your product solves, or what amazing outcome it delivers, and for whom.

Put that at the top of your homepage.

If you have videos that answer visitors' questions, by all means add them to the site. Just put them a little further down on the homepage. Maybe place them deeper in the funnel: on a Product page, or How It Works page. But remember that not everyone wants to watch them, and not everyone can. So make sure the information they contain can easily be found in text form.

Bonus: Looking to get more views of the videos you've added elsewhere on your site? Spell out, ideally in the copy that surrounds them, how they're helpful—and how long they are. ("See how it works in 30 seconds" is way more inviting than "Watch the video.")

AFTERWORD

Your website doesn't suck anymore

Congratulations! You did it.

If you've made it this far, your website most decidedly does not suck—or at a minimum, you've got a helpful to-do list that will ensure it won't for much longer. So, now what?

There are a few possibilities to consider.

You might want to start experimenting

You've addressed the biggest issues with your site, and I hope you're seeing improved results already. But that doesn't mean there are no further gains to be had.

Embarking on a disciplined program of experimentation (sometimes called conversion rate optimization) will uncover even more opportunities to increase the percentage of visitors who purchase (or sign up, or reach out) over time.

It requires skills in design, development, and data analysis. You will probably want to bring in help. But it's a fun and informative way to continually improve business results while learning more about your visitors—and making sure your site doesn't get worse over time.

You might want to focus on acquisition

As you're no doubt well aware by now, this book is focused on *conversion*: getting visitors to do what you want them to do once they're on your site. Now that you've dialed that in, it may make sense to shift your priority to *acquisition*: getting more visitors to come to the site in the first place.

This could mean investing in search engine optimization (SEO), social media marketing, hosting events, cold outreach, or all of the above. You might also consider spending money on paid advertising.

Whether it's time or cash you're putting in, the fixes and improvements you've made on your site should make every additional hour and every additional dollar pay off even more. Success is built upon a non-sucky website.

You should definitely conduct customer research

The two suggestions above (experimentation and acquisition) are optional. You could do one, or the other, or possibly both.

Then again, you might do neither. Maybe your site gets as much traffic as it needs, and enough of those visitors are taking action to leave your business in a good place for now.

That's okay, too! You're under no obligation to continue tweaking your website until the heat death of the universe, and there's no iron law that says you must maintain an ongoing ad budget. Take some time off, or work on something other than digital marketing.

But customer research is one practice you should never consider finished.

It can take many forms: user testing, on-site surveys, customer interviews. Each method gives a different kind of insight into your customers' mindset and behavior.

It doesn't have to be complicated, or expensive. A few 20-minute interviews will tell you tons about how your visitors think about your product and the problem it solves. You can run a user test for a few hundred dollars. It only takes a few minutes to launch an on-site survey, and a few hours to analyze the results.

You can tailor your customer research to fit your budget and to chase down specific questions about your site(say, identifying points of doubt or confusion). But you've got to do it, and on an ongoing basis, lest you slip back into suckage territory.

This book has given you an understanding of universal principles when it comes to web design, but conducting your own research will give you insights that are *specific to your customers*.

That knowledge will lead to further website improvements, more effective acquisition strategy, and a better product overall.

I can help

Whatever you decide to do next, you'll find additional info, guides, recommendations, and more on the website for this book.

Just visit https://yourwebsitesucks.fyi/book-resources.

That page will also tell you how to get in touch with me. I'd love to hear about your own website journey, so please don't hesitate to reach out. That would not suck at all.

ACKNOWLEDGMENTS

First and most importantly I want to thank Misty, François, Robocop, and Sox for creating the warm, loving, and entertaining environment that allowed me to spend a couple hundred hours ranting about websites without losing touch with reality.

Much appreciation to Andrew Anderson, Tim Duke, and Ben Labay, three experts who have generously explained simple concepts to me over and over until they finally clicked.

I'm eternally grateful to Vince Amatuzzi, Nichole Elizabeth DeMere, Shrubrank Mukhiya, Sílvia Pinho, Marjorie Turner Hollman, Kate Warwick, and the many anonymous beta readers who trudged through early drafts, offering encouragement and gentle pointers to the clumsy and incoherent bits.

Many mahalos to Rob Fitzpatrick, Adam Rosen, and Saeah Lee Wood. I leaned heavily on their writing and publishing expertise throughout the entire process. (The good parts of this book are because of their input, and the bad parts are because I stubbornly refused to listen.)

And of course a big thanks to *all* the supportive friends, readers, and internet randos who've kept me going for the past year and a half. If you've read this far, that means you, too.

.

Made in the USA
Columbia, SC
13 September 2023

22827732R00076